A true friend is a pearl.

Jean de La Fontaine

Other books in the *"Language of"* Series...

Blue Mountain Arts®

It's Great to Have a Brother like You
It's Great to Have a Sister like You
Love and Wishes for You, Daughter
The Language of a Mother's Love
The Language of Brides
The Language of Courage and Inner Strength
The Language of Dance
The Language of Friendship
The Language of Happiness
The Language of Love
The Language of Marriage
The Language of Parenting
The Language of Positive Thinking
The Language of Prayer
The Language of Recovery
The Language of Success
The Language of Teaching
The Language of Teenagers
Thoughts to Share with a Wonderful Daughter
Thoughts to Share with a Wonderful Father
Thoughts to Share with a Wonderful Mother
Thoughts to Share with a Wonderful Son
Words of Comfort ...for You in Your Time of Loss
You Will Always Have an Angel Watching Over You

The "Language of" Series...

Thoughts to Share with a
WONDERFUL
FRIEND

*A Blue Mountain Arts® Collection
About the Special Joys of Friendship*

Edited by Gwendolyn Gray

Blue Mountain Press ™

SPS Studios, Inc., Boulder, Colorado

We wish to thank Susan Polis Schutz for permission to reprint the following poems: "You Are Always My Friend" and "You have known me...." Copyright © 1982, 1984 by Stephen Schutz and Susan Polis Schutz. All rights reserved.

Library of Congress Control Number: 2002093188
ISBN: 0-88396-688-3

ACKNOWLEDGMENTS appear on page 48.

Certain trademarks are used under license.

Manufactured in Thailand.
First Printing: 2003

 This book is printed on recycled paper.

SPS Studios, Inc.

P.O. Box 4549, Boulder, Colorado 80306

Contents

(Authors listed in order of first appearance)

A Friend Is One of Life's Most Beautiful Gifts

A friend is a person you can trust,
who won't turn away from you;
a friend will be there
when you really need someone,
and will come to you when they need help.
A friend will listen to you
even when they don't understand
or agree with your feelings;
a friend will never try to change you,
but appreciates you for who you are.
A friend doesn't expect too much
or give too little;
a friend is someone you can share
dreams, hopes, and feelings with.
A friend is a person you can think of
and suddenly smile;
a friend doesn't have to be told
that they are special,
because they know you feel that way.

A friend will accept your attitudes,
ideas, and emotions,
even when their own are different,
and will hold your hand when you're scared.
A friend will be honest with you
even when it might hurt,
and will forgive you
for the mistakes you make.
A friend can never disappoint you,
and will support you and share in your glory.
A friend shares responsibility
when you have doubts.
A friend always remembers
the little things you've done,
the times you've shared,
and the talks you've had.
A friend will bend over backwards
to help you pick up the pieces
when your world falls apart.
A friend is one of life's
most beautiful gifts.

 Luann Auciello

You Are Always
My Friend

You are always my friend
when I am happy
or when I am sad
when I am all alone
or when I am with people
You are always my friend
if I see you today
or if I see you
    a year from now
if I talk to you today
or if I talk to you
    a year from now
You are always my friend
    and though through the years
we will change
it doesn't matter what I do
or it doesn't matter what you do
Throughout our lifetime
you are always my friend

— Susan Polis Schutz

Friends are angels sent
down to earth to make
good days and to help
us find our way.

— Ashley Rice

Our friends are the continuous threads
that help hold our lives together.

— Sarah Ban Breathnach

I get by with a little help from my friends.

John Lennon and Paul McCartney

The Best Source of Happiness

Friendship cheers like a sunbeam; charms like a good story; inspires like a brave leader; binds like a golden chain; guides like a heavenly vision.

Newell D. Hillis

My friend peers in on me with merry
Wise face, and though the sky stays dim,
The very light of day, the very
Sun's self come in with him.

Algernon Charles Swinburne

I see no sunshine but in the face of a friend.

Alexander Pope

It is a sweet thing, friendship — a dear balm;
A happy and auspicious bird of calm
Which rides o'er life's ever-tumultuous ocean.

Percy Bysshe Shelley

Friendship is a gift, continually giving happiness. It is strong and supportive, and few things in all the world will ever compare with the joy that comes from its wonderful bond.

Mia Evans

Life has no pleasure higher or nobler than that of friendship.

Samuel Johnson

Of all the means to insure happiness throughout the whole of life, by far the most important is the acquisition of friends.

Epicurus

The more we nurture our friendships, the greater the happiness that comes our way.

Mary Lou Retton

Dividing Troubles...

If the while I think on thee, dear friend,
All losses are restored and sorrows end.

— William Shakespeare

For there is no man that imparteth his joys to his friend,
but he joyeth the more, and no man that imparteth his
griefs to his friend, but he grieveth the less.

— Francis Bacon

Now friendship possesses many splendid
advantages, but of course the finest thing
of all about it is that it sends a ray of good
hope into the future, and keeps our hearts
from faltering or falling by the wayside.

 — Cicero

... Doubling Joys

When clouds and darkness veil the skies,
And sorrow's blast blows loud and chill,
Friendship shall like a rainbow rise,
And softly whisper — peace, be still.

— Lucretia Maria Davidson

Friendship is a sheltering tree.

— Samuel Taylor Coleridge

This life on earth's a poison tree,
And yet with two fruits sweet:
Ambrosia of poesy,
And joy when true friends meet.

 Kâlidâsa

Always Giving Their Best...

My definition of an ideal friend is a
person who would do anything for you
and for whom you'd do anything in return.

Sandy Maxx

One of the world's most
amazing miracles is how far
our true friends will go to give
us the gifts we really need.
And as only our truest friends
could, they often give, without
being asked, the thing we most
need but could never ask for.

 Ellen Jacob

One of the best things about having a true friend is that no matter how far away they are, how long it has been since you've spoken, or how much has happened in each of your lives, they are never really gone from your heart. They always remain a part of your life — whether you see them every day or only when they drift in and out through the years.

Jane Andrews

Friendship is the greatest bond in the world.

 Jeremy Taylor

Friends are together when they are separated, they are rich when they are poor, strong when they are weak, and — a thing even harder to explain — they live on after they have died, so great is the honor that follows them, so vivid the memory, so poignant the sorrow.

 Cicero

The Comfort of Friends

Friends are like home. They're that place we can come to relax, put up our feet, have some fun, and find relief from the rest of the world. We know that with them we can cut loose, be ourselves, and never worry about being judged.

— Noelle Cleary and Dini von Mueffling

What a great blessing is a friend with a heart so trusty you may safely bury all your secrets in it, whose conscience you may fear less than your own, who can relieve your cares by his conversation, your doubts by his counsels, your sadness by his good humor, and whose very looks give you comfort.

— Seneca

There are certain people whom we are
so close to and who are
so dear to our hearts
There are certain people who can
bring us a ray of happiness with just a smile
and who can make us feel better
just by listening and showing that they care
There are certain people who can
make our day with a kind word
They can bring us hope when
our hearts are low
They are a part of who we are, and
they make a difference in our lives
They offer us the comfort of knowing
someone understands
and the satisfaction of knowing
we have something to believe in
They are people like you
who are so deserving
of such admiration and praise...
for it's friends like you who are
forever loved so dearly

Shannon M. Lester

Brought Together by Destiny

When you least expect it, a common thread — golden, at that — begins to weave together the fabric of friendship.

— Mary Kay Shanley

Whatever be the method by which a true friendship is formed, whether the growth of time or the birth of sudden sympathy, there seems, on looking back, to have been an element of necessity. It is a sort of predestined spiritual relationship. We speak of a man meeting his fate, and we speak truly. When we look back we see it to be like destiny; life converged to life, and there was no getting out of it even if we wished it. It is not that we made a choice, but that the choice made us.

— Hugh Black

Two may talk together under the same roof
for many years, yet never really meet; and
two others at first speech are old friends.

— Mary Catherwood

Our friend is an unconscious part
Of every true beat of our heart.

— Lucy Larcom

In the friendship I speak of, our souls
mingle and blend with each other so
completely that they efface the seam
that joined them, and cannot find it
again. If you press me to tell why I
loved him, I feel that this cannot be
expressed, except by answering:
Because it was he, because it was I.

— Michel de Montaigne

United by Friendship

Friends are true twins in soul; they sympathize in everything, and have the same love and aversion.

— William Penn

Two sturdy oaks I mean, which side by side,
  Withstand the winter's storm,
  And spite of wind and tide,
  Grow up the meadow's pride,
    For both are strong

Above they barely touch, but undermined
  Down to their deepest source,
  Admiring you shall find
  Their roots are intertwined
    Insep'rably.

— Henry David Thoreau

So we grew together,
Like a double cherry, seeming parted,
But yet an union in partition,
Two lovely berries moulded on one stem;
So with two seeming bodies, but one heart.

 William Shakespeare

Friendship — one heart in two bodies.

 Joseph Zabara

Are we not like two volumes of one book?

 Marceline Desbordes-Valmore

Lifelong Friends

A lifelong friend
is one who enters your life
at a time when they are needed most.
Though you may not understand it,
between you and a lifelong friend
there will be an instant bonding
and a realization
that this person was brought to you,
not only to fill an emptiness
or assist you in time of need,
but to form an eternal friendship.
A lifelong friend
is a friend who knows you like no other,
who is so much a part of you
that distance does not cause separation.

They will hurt when you hurt
and feel joy when you are joyous.
They know your imperfections,
and they accept them as a part of you.
Though they may not agree
with your decisions,
lifelong friends will support you completely
in everything you do.
They respect you and your right
to make your life what you want it to be.
When all the others have come and gone,
this friend will be with you;
even if your world falls apart,
they will be there to build it back up
better and stronger than before.
This is the essence of lifelong friendship.

 Lisa VanEllen

❧ A Friend Is... ❧

...what the heart needs all the time.

❧ Henry Van Dyke

...a smile amid dark frowns — a gentle tone
Among rude voices, a beloved light,
A solitude, a refuge, a delight.

❧ Percy Bysshe Shelley

...a shoulder to lean on
   when you need support,
a pat on the back when you do well,
and a sympathetic ear when you fail.
A friend is a person you can laugh with
   about everything,
you can cry with, without shame,
and whom you trust completely.
A friend is a partner in life
   and a part of you always.

❧ Brian Bindschadler

...someone who is always ready and willing to share in your laughter, your tears, your dreams, your failures, your secrets, and your celebrations.

— Jane Andrews

...another self, to whom we impart our most secret thoughts, who partakes of our joy, and comforts us in our affliction; add to this, that his company is an everlasting pleasure to us.

Bidpai

...far dearer,
Than all this earth's fine gold!

— Simon Dach

...a one-in-a-million find,
the pot of gold at the end of the rainbow,
a treasure that gives you wealth untold.

Vickie M. Worsham

A Special Friend
Is a Rare Find

A special friend is...
someone who shares
your joy and happiness,
someone who cares enough
to show love and kindness,
someone who is a comfort
to spend time with,
someone who is honest
and thoughtful.

A special friend is a wonderful gift...
someone who offers understanding
when life is difficult,
someone whose smile is enough
to brighten any day,
someone who accepts you
and is glad that you are you,
someone who forgets mistakes
and is gentle and trusting.
You are this special friend to me.

Donna Levine Small

A true friend is a pearl.

Jean de La Fontaine

There are rare people in this world
who are always there to listen
with a smile and a loving, open heart.
You are one of
those rare people...
How fortunate I am
that you are my friend!

Andrea L. Hines

No Greater Treasure

People who have warm friends are healthier and happier than those who have none. A single real friend is a treasure worth more than gold or precious stones. Money can buy many things, good and evil. All the wealth of the world could not buy you a friend or pay you for the loss of one.

C. D. Prentice

Fortune can't take away what you give friends: that wealth stays yours forever.

Martial

You meet your friend, your face brightens —
you have struck gold.

Kassia

Being her friend, I do not covet gold,
    Save for a royal gift to give her pleasure;
To sit wth her, and have her hand to hold,
    Is wealth, I think, surpassing minted treasure.

 John Masefield

A friend is a living treasure, and if you have one,
you have one of the most valuable gifts in life.

 Collin McCarty

❀ *Side by Side...* ❀

True friends,
Like ivy and the wall,
Both stand together,
And together fall.

❀— Thomas Carlyle

Friendship's like music; two strings tuned alike,
Will both stir, though but only one you strike.

❀ Francis Quarles

Friends do not live in harmony merely,
as some say, but in melody.

 Henry David Thoreau

... Through It All *

You have known me
in good and
bad times
You have seen me
when I was happy
and when I was sad
You have listened to me
when what I said was intelligent
and when I talked nonsense
You have been with me
when we had fun
and when we were miserable

You have watched me
laugh
and cry
You have understood me
when I knew what I was doing
and when I made mistakes
Thank you for
believing in me
for supporting me
and for always being ready
to share thoughts together
You are a perfect friend

— Susan Polis Schutz

The glory of friendship... is the
spirited inspiration that comes
to one when he discovers that
someone else believes in him
and is willing to trust him with
his friendship.

Ralph Waldo Emerson

A friend is the one who will always be
beside you, through all the laughter, and
through each and every tear. A friend is
the one thing you can always rely on; the
someone you can always open up to; the
one wonderful person who always believes
in you in a way that no one else seems to.

Collin McCarty

When two people have shared
as much as you and I have;
when they've opened up their hearts,
shared their dreams,
thoughts, and fears;
when two people
believe in one another
and are always sincere
to each other;
when they
have trusted one another
with the truth
that lies within —
then you can be sure
that they're friends for life...
just like
you and me.

                              Zoe Dellous

Friends Only See
the Best in Each Other

They came to tell your faults to me,
They named them over one by one;
I laughed aloud when they were done,
I knew them all so well before —
Oh, they were blind, too blind to see
Your faults had made me love you more.

— Sara Teasdale

Our friends see the best in us, and by
that very fact call forth the best from us.

— Hugh Black

The depth of a friendship — how much it means to
us... depends, at least in part, upon how many parts
of ourselves a friend sees, shares and validates.

— Lillian Rubin

Your friend is the man who knows
all about you, and still likes you.

— Elbert Hubbard

Two persons cannot long be friends if they cannot
forgive each other's little failings.

— Jean de La Bruyère

Every man should have a fair-sized cemetery
in which to bury the faults of his friends.

— Henry Ward Beecher

Perfection is not essential to friendship.

— Alexander Smith

I always felt that the great high privilege,
relief, and comfort of friendship was that
one had to explain nothing.

Katherine Mansfield

Friendship needs no studied phrases,
    Polished face, or winning wiles;
Friendship deals no lavish praises,
    Friendship dons no surface smiles.

Friendship follows Nature's diction,
    Shuns the blandishments of art,
Boldly severs truth from fiction,
    Speaks the language of the heart.

Anonymous

Silence

'Tis better to sit here beside the sea,
Here on the spray-kissed beach,
In silence, that between such friends as we
Is full of deepest speech.

Paul Laurence Dunbar

When your friend... is silent your heart ceases
not to listen to his heart;

For without words, in friendship, all thoughts, all
desires, all expectations are born and shared, with joy
that is unacclaimed.

Kahlil Gibran

You can tell when two people are close friends. They have a strange
way of finishing each other's sentences, beginning to laugh about an
old joke long before the punch line, communicating with their eyes, or
contentedly sitting in silence with a sense of complete understanding.

Jane Andrews

Cherished Memories

For every time we have grabbed our sides
   while laughing together,
For every time we have shed a tear of
   compassion for each other's heartaches,
For every time we have run to each other
   bursting to share exciting news,
For every time we have felt joy and strength
   from our closeness, I thank you.
I am glad you are always there for me to turn to.
And I am especially glad for the memories we share.

— Susan Hickman Sater

When old friends speak of the past
after the years apart, lives so different,
                                    how well
they seem to know us, still,
after such a long time, better than our families,
our lovers.
         So much of ourselves that we had forgotten
alive in them still.

— August Kleinzahler

W hen we examine sunlight streaming through a window, we notice the dust motes sparkling, moving, dancing in the air. So it is with our memories of our friends and their memories of us. We may not even know they are there, unless the full light of our consciousness comes to rest on a memory. But they are always present, dancing, moving, swirling in our thoughts and around and through our souls.

 — Carmen Renee Berry and Tamara Traeder

A friend hears the song in my heart
and sings it to me when my memory fails.

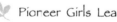 Pioneer Girls Leaders' Handbook

R emember the time
Before the wax hardened,
When everyone was like a seal.
Each of us bears the imprint
Of a friend met along the way;
In each the trace of each.

Primo Levi

Friendship

Each of us has a hidden place
Somewhere deep within ourselves;
A place where we go to get away,
To think things through,
To be alone, to be ourselves.

This unique place, where we confront our deepest
  feelings,
Becomes a storehouse of all our hopes,
All our needs, all our dreams,
And even our unspoken fears.
It encompasses the essence of who we are and what we
  want to be.

But now and then, whether by chance or design,
Someone discovers a way into this place we thought
    was ours alone.
And we allow that person to see, to feel and to share
All the reason, all the uncertainty
And all the emotion we've stored up there.

That person adds new perspective to our hidden realm,
Then quietly settles down in his own corner of our
    special place,
Where a bit of himself will stay forever.

And we call that person a friend.

Carol Elaine Faivre-Scott

The Bond of a Lifetime

A true friend is forever a friend.

— George Macdonald

The silver friend knows your present and the gold friend knows all of your past dirt and glories. Once in a blue moon there's someone who knows it all, someone who knows and accepts you unconditionally, someone who's there for life.

— Jill McCorkle

The growth of true friendship may be a lifelong affair.

— Sarah Orne Jewett

I want to be your friend
For ever and ever without break or decay.
When the hills are all flat
And the rivers are all dry,
When it lightens and thunders in winter,
When it rains and snows in summer,
When Heaven and Earth mingle —
Not till then will I part from you.

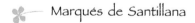 — Chinese Oath

I ask you and I urge you
To keep forever
Your friend a friend
In truth.

— Marqués de Santillana

Some Friends
Are Forever

Sometimes in life,
you find a special friend:
someone who changes your life
by being a part of it.
Someone who makes you laugh
until you can't stop;
someone who makes you believe
that there really is good in the world.
Someone who convinces you
that there is an unlocked door
just waiting for you to open it.
This is forever friendship.

When you're down,
and the world seems dark and empty,
your forever friend lifts you up in spirit
and makes that dark and empty world
suddenly seem bright and full.

Your forever friend gets you through
the hard times, the sad times,
and the confused times.
If you turn and walk away,
your forever friend follows.
If you lose your way,
your forever friend guides you
and cheers you on.
Your forever friend holds your hand
and tells you that
everything is going to be okay.
And if you find such a friend,
you feel happy and complete,
because you need not worry.
You have a forever friend for life,
and forever has no end.

 Laurieann Kelly

Friends Are the Most Special
People in Life

Friends are cherished people
whom we carry in our hearts
wherever we go in life.
We spend a lot of time together,
getting to know one another
and sharing one another's lives.
And no matter where we go,
we always remember
the wonderful people who touched our lives
and who loved us and helped us
learn more about ourselves.

We always remember
the people who stayed by us
when we had to face difficult times
and with whom we felt safe enough
to reveal our true selves.
Friends are the unforgettable people
we dream and plan
great futures with,
who accept us as we are
and encourage us to become
all that we want to be.

My friend,
no matter where we go in life,
you will always be close to me,
and I will always be your friend.

Donna Levine Small

ACKNOWLEDGMENTS

We gratefully acknowledge the permission granted by the following authors, publishers, and authors' representatives to reprint poems or excerpts from their publications.

Penguin Books Ltd. for "A true friend is…" from LA FONTAINE: SELECTED FABLES by Jean de La Fontaine, translated by James Michie. Copyright © 1979 by James Michie. All rights reserved.

Warner Books, Inc., for "Our friends are the continuous…" from SIMPLE ABUNDANCE by Sarah Ban Breathnach. Copyright © 1995 by Sarah Ban Breathnach. All rights reserved.

Sony/ATV Music Publishing, Inc., for "I get by with a little help…" from "With a Little Help from My Friends" by John Lennon and Paul McCartney. Copyright © 1967 (Renewed) by Sony/ATV Tunes LLC. All rights administered by Sony/ATV Music Publishing, 8 Music Square West, Nashville, TN 37203. All rights reserved. Used by permission.

Broadway Books, a division of Random House, Inc., for "The more we nurture…" from MARY LOU RETTON'S GATEWAY TO HAPPINESS by Mary Lou Retton and David Bender. Copyright © 2000 by MLR Entertainment, Inc. and Momentum Partners, Inc. All rights reserved.

Andrews McMeel Publishing for "My definition of an ideal friend…" by Sandy Maxx and "One of the world's most amazing…" by Ellen Jacob from YOU'RE THE BEST FRIEND EVER by Ellen Jacob. Copyright © 2001 by Ellen Jacob. All rights reserved.

Grove/Atlantic, Inc., for "Friends are like home…" from THE ART AND POWER OF BEING A LADY by Noelle Cleary and Dini von Mueffling. Copyright © 2001 by Noelle Cleary and Dini von Mueffling. All rights reserved.

Sta-Kris, Inc., for "When you least expect it…" from SHE TAUGHT ME TO EAT ARTICHOKES by Mary Kay Shanley. Copyright © 1993 by Mary Kay Shanley. All rights reserved.

Brian Bindschadler for "A friend is a shoulder to lean on…." Copyright © 2002 by Brian Bindschadler. All rights reserved.

Andrea L. Hines for "There are rare people…." Copyright © 2002 by Andrea L. Hines. All rights reserved.

The Society of Authors as the Literary Representative of the Estate of John Masefield for "Being Her Friend" from POEMS by John Masefield. Copyright © 1941 by MacMillan Company. All rights reserved.

Scribner, an imprint of Simon & Schuster Adult Publishing Group, for "They came to tell your faults…" from THE COLLECTED POETRY OF SARA TEASDALE by Sara Teasdale. Copyright © 1935 by the MacMillan Company. All rights reserved.

Lillian B. Rubin for "The depth of a friendship…" from JUST FRIENDS, published by Harper & Row Publishers. Copyright © 1985 by Lillian B. Rubin. All rights reserved.

Alfred A. Knopf and the Gibran National Committee, Beirut, Lebanon, for "When your friend… is silent…" from THE PROPHET by Kahlil Gibran. Copyright © 1923 by Kahlil Gibran. Copyright renewed 1951 by Administrators C.T.A. of Kahlil Gibran Estate and Mary G. Gibran. All rights reserved.

August Kleinzahler for "When old friends speak…" from EARTHQUAKE WEATHER published by Moyer Bell Limited. Copyright © 1989 by August Kleinzahler. All rights reserved.

Wildcat Canyon Press, a division of Circulus Publishing Group Inc., for "When we examine sunlight streaming…" from GIRLFRIENDS by Carmen Renee Berry and Tamara Traeder. Copyright © 1995 by Carmen Renee Berry and Tamara C. Traeder. All rights reserved.

Faber and Faber, Inc., an affiliate of Farrar, Strauss and Giroux, LLC., for "Remember the time…" from PRIMO LEVI: COLLECTED POEMS by Primo Levi, translated by Ruth Feldman and Brian Swann. Copyright © 1988 by Ruth Feldman and Brian Swann. All rights reserved.

Carol Elaine Faivre-Scott for "Friendship." Copyright © 2002 by Carol Elaine Faivre-Scott. All rights reserved.

Jill McCorkle for "The silver friend knows your present…" from BETWEEN FRIENDS, published by Houghton Mifflin Company. Copyright © 1994 by Jill McCorkle. All rights reserved.

A careful effort has been made to trace the ownership of selections used in this anthology in order to obtain permission to reprint copyrighted material and give proper credit to the copyright owners. If any error or omission has occurred, it is completely inadvertent, and we would like to make corrections in future editions provided that written notification is made to the publisher:

SPS STUDIOS, INC., P.O. Box 4549, Boulder, Colorado 80306.